This book belongs to!

@Jerryloubooks
@contactJerryLou
@JerryLou_books

1.brown   2.purple   3.orange

4.yellow   5.black   6.blue

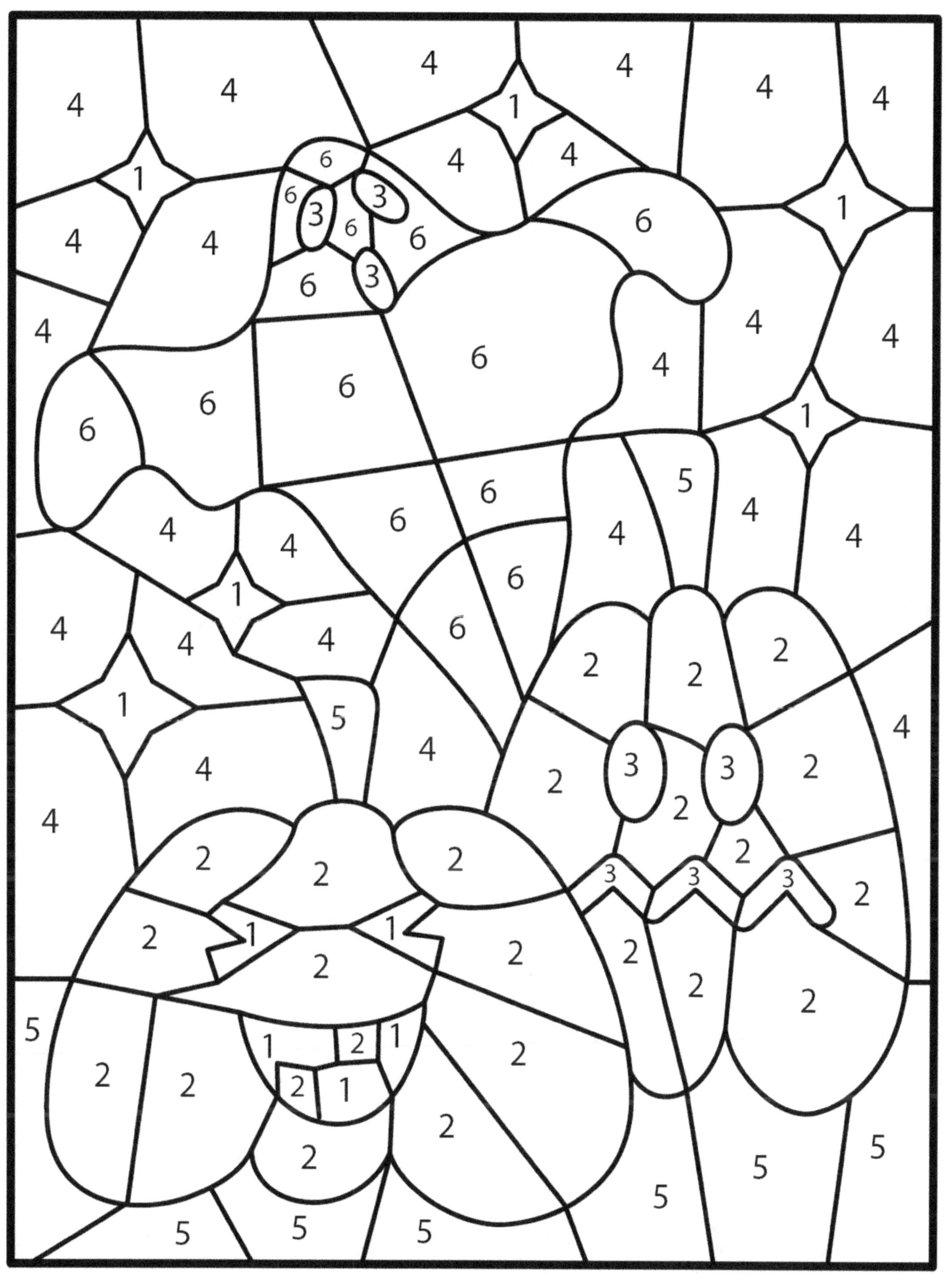

1.yellow 2.orange 3.black
4.blue 5.green 6.gray

HAPPY
HALLOWEEN

TRICK
OR
TREAT!

1.beige
2.yeloow
3.orange
4. blue
5. purple
6. green

1.light blue	4.orange	7.white
2.blue	5.light orange	8.blue
3.purple	6.black	9.pink
	10.red